More Christmas Origami

by Ruth Owen

PowerKiDS press

New York

Published in 2015 by
The Rosen Publishing Group, Inc.
29 East 21st Street, New York, NY 10010

Library of Congress Cataloging-in-Publication Data
Owen, Ruth.
More Christmas origami / by Ruth Owen.
p. cm. — (Holiday origami)
Includes index.
ISBN 978-1-4777-5707-9 (pbk.)
ISBN 978-1-4777-5708-6 (6-pack)
ISBN 978-1-4777-5706-2 (library binding)
1. Origami — Juvenile literature. 2. Christmas decorations — Juvenile literature.
I. Owen, Ruth, 1967-. II. Title.
TT870.O94 2015
736.982—d23

Produced for Rosen by Ruby Tuesday Books Ltd
Editor for Ruby Tuesday Books Ltd: Mark J. Sachner
US Editor: Sara Antill
Designer: Emma Randall

Photo Credits:
Cover, 1, 3, 5, 7, 12, 16, 20, 24, 28 © Shutterstock
Origami models © Ruby Tuesday Books Ltd.

Manufactured in the United States of America

CPSIA Compliance Information: Batch # CW15PK: For Further Information contact
Rosen Publishing, New York, New York at 1-800-237-9932

Contents

Origami in Action

If you love making crafts and gifts for your friends and family, you will love **origami**! Using colored paper or recycled gift-wrapping paper you can make origami Christmas decorations and **unique** gifts.

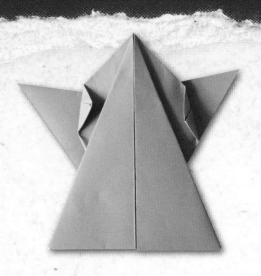

Origami is the art of folding paper to make small **sculptures**, or models. This wonderful art form gets its name from the Japanese words "ori," which means "folding," and "kami," which means "paper." People have been making origami models in Japan for hundreds of years.

If you've never tried origami before, don't be nervous! This book will show you how to make mini-Christmas trees, stars, a paper Santa, a wreath, angels, and even a reindeer! So get some paper and let's get folding!

Get Folding!

Before you get started on your Christmas origami models, here are some tips.

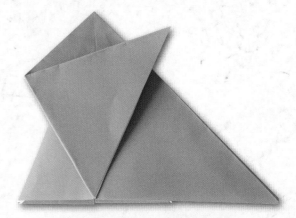

Tip 1

Read all the instructions carefully and look at the pictures. Make sure you understand what's required before you begin a fold. Don't rush; be patient. Work slowly and carefully.

Tip 2

Folding a piece of paper sounds easy, but it can be tricky to get neat, accurate folds. The more you practice, the easier it becomes.

Tip 3

If an instruction says "crease," make the crease as flat as possible. The flatter the creases, the better the model. You can make a sharp crease by running a plastic ruler along the edge of the paper.

Tip 4

Sometimes, at first, your models may look a little crumpled. Don't give up! The more models you make, the better you will get at folding and creasing.

When it comes to origami, practice makes perfect!

Take a look at this colorful Christmas tree and complicated origami star. These models were made by experienced origami model makers. Keep practicing and you could soon be making difficult models like these!

Some of the origami models in this book can be used to create homemade Christmas cards. Try glueing Santa or some angels to a piece of cardboard. Add a bow and you will have a very special and personal Christmas greeting.

Origami Angel

Angels are a very important part of the Christmas story. An angel named Gabriel appeared to Mary and told her she would give birth to Jesus, the Son of God. When Jesus was born in a stable in Bethlehem, an angel appeared to shepherds who were tending their sheep nearby. With great celebration, the angel announced to the shepherds that a Savior had been born.

Today, angels are a much-loved holiday decoration. Many people place an angel on the top of their Christmas tree.

These origami angels are very simple to make. You will quickly be able to create a host of beautiful paper angels to decorate your home.

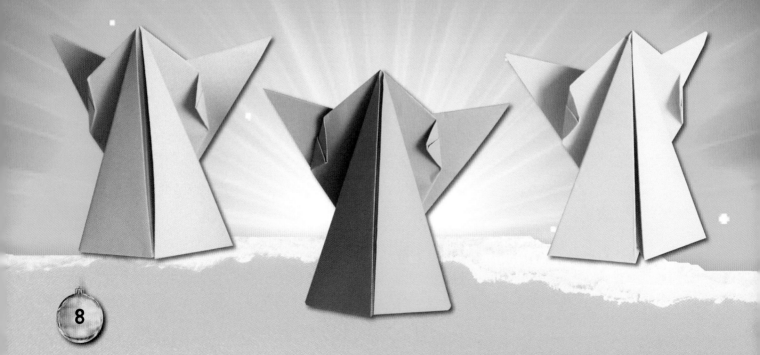

To make origami angels, you will need:

Scissors

Sheets of origami paper in colors
of your choice

(Origami paper is sometimes colored on both sides or white on one side.)

STEP 1:
Place the paper colored-side down. Fold in half from side to side, crease, and unfold. Then fold down from top to bottom, crease, and unfold.

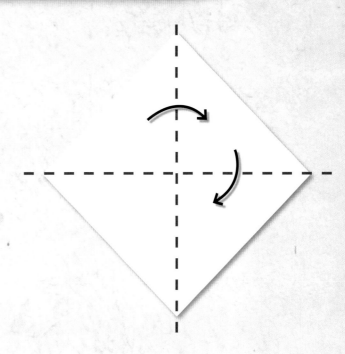

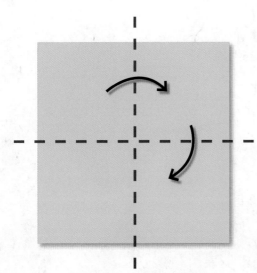

STEP 2:
Turn the paper over. Fold in half from side to side, crease, and unfold. Then fold down from top to bottom, crease, and unfold.

STEP 3:

Place the paper colored-side down. Using the creases you've just made, collapse and fold up the paper to form a flattened triangle by bringing A in to meet B, point C down to meet point D, and point E down to meet point F.

As you collapse and fold up the paper, it should look like this.

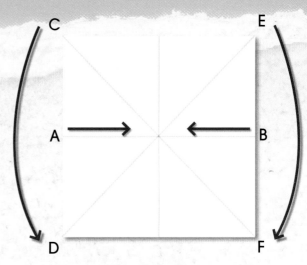

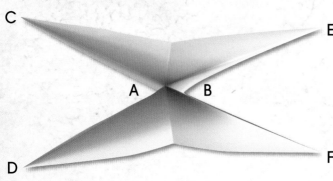

Flattened triangle

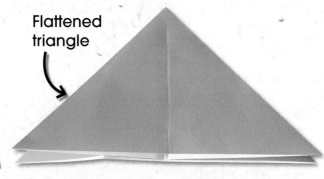

STEP 4:

Take the right-hand corner of the triangle and fold it into the center, and crease. Repeat on the left-hand side.

STEP 5:

Trim off the two points at the bottom of the model.

STEP 6:

Turn the model over. To make the angel's wings, fold up the left-hand corner of the triangle, and crease well. Then fold the wing back along the dotted line, and crease well.

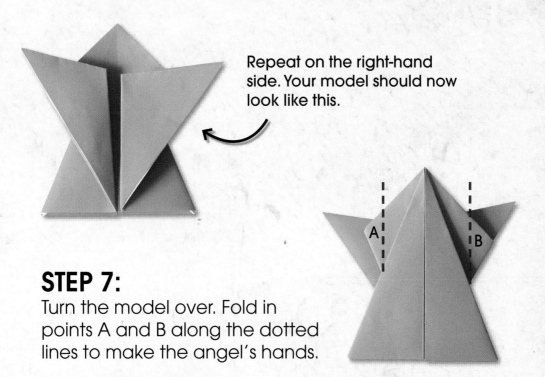

Repeat on the right-hand side. Your model should now look like this.

STEP 7:

Turn the model over. Fold in points A and B along the dotted lines to make the angel's hands.

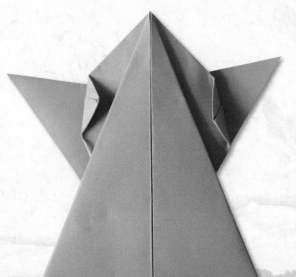

Your origami angel is complete. Gently open out the bottom of the model to help it stand.

Origami Christmas Star

Stars are another very special Christmas **symbol**.

In the Christmas story, a bright star appears in the sky when Jesus is born. The star leads the three wise men to Bethlehem to the birthplace of Jesus. The star is sometimes called *The Star of Bethlehem.*

In this project, you will learn how to create a six-pointed Christmas star. You can use origami paper or scraps of Christmas gift-wrapping paper to make your model. You can even use your star model as a decoration for the top of your Christmas tree.

Scissors

Sheets of origami paper in your color choices,
or pieces of Christmas wrapping paper

(Origami paper is sometimes colored on both sides or white on one side.)

STEP 1:
To make a star that's approximately
3 inches (8 cm) across, you will need
six small squares of paper that
are 3 inches (8 cm) square.

STEP 2:
Take one square of paper. Place
it colored-side down. Fold in half
from side to side, crease, and
unfold. Then fold down from top
to bottom, crease, and unfold.

STEP 3:
Turn the paper over. Fold in half from
side to side, crease, and unfold.
Then fold down from top to bottom,
crease, and unfold.

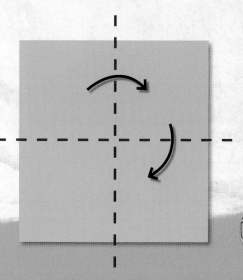

STEP 4:

Place the paper colored-side down. Using the creases you've just made, collapse and fold up the paper to form a flattened triangle by bringing A in to meet B, point C down to meet point D, and point E down to meet point F.

As you collapse and fold up the paper, it should look like this.

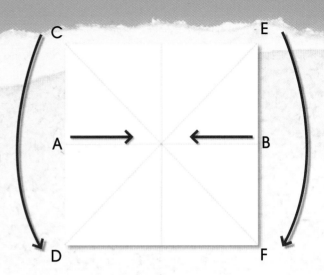

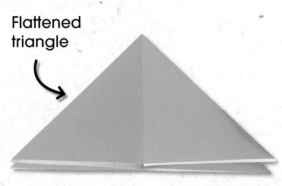

Flattened triangle

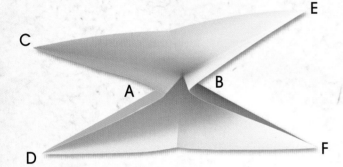

STEP 5:

Repeat steps 2 to 4 with the other five squares of paper.

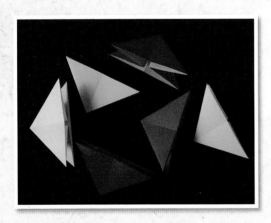

STEP 6:

Now take two triangles and gently slide the points of one triangle inside the points of the other, so that the two triangles slot together tightly.

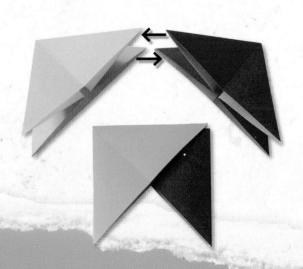

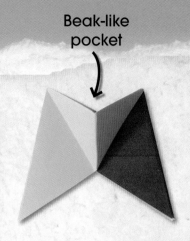

Pocket

Beak-like pocket

STEP 7:

At the top of your model, there will be a pocket. Gently squeeze the two triangles together so that the pocket pops open. Keep gently squeezing and opening out the pocket, creasing as you go, so it becomes beak-like.

STEP 8:

Now repeat Step 7 with a third triangle.

Beak-like pocket

STEP 9:

Keep slotting the triangles together. Open out each of the pockets on the edges of the model, squeezing and creasing them to form beak-like pockets.

Beak-like pockets

STEP 10:

Once all six triangles are slotted together, complete the star by slotting the points of triangle six into triangle one. This is tricky, so work slowly, and be patient!

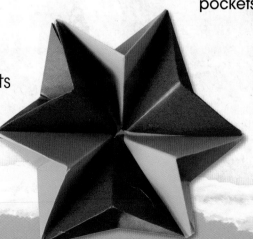

Origami Christmas Tree

We all know that Christmas has truly arrived once it's time to decorate the tree! And this year, why just have one tree when it's so easy to create a forest of mini origami trees?

These tiny trees are perfect as a table decoration. You can also give them to the adults you know who work in offices to brighten up their desks during the holiday season.

These trees also squash flat, so you can pop them inside your Xmas cards and send everyone you know their own origami tree.

To make origami Christmas trees, you will need:

Sheets of origami paper in shades of green

(Origami paper is sometimes colored on both sides or white on one side.)

STEP 1:

Place the paper white-side down. Fold in half from side to side, crease, and unfold. Then fold down from top to bottom, crease, and unfold.

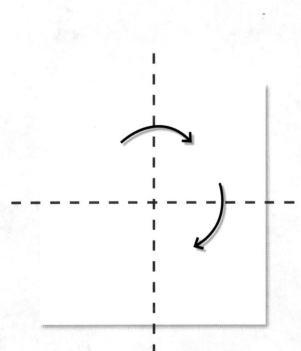

STEP 2:

Turn the paper over. Fold in half from side to side, crease, and unfold. Then fold down from top to bottom, crease, and unfold.

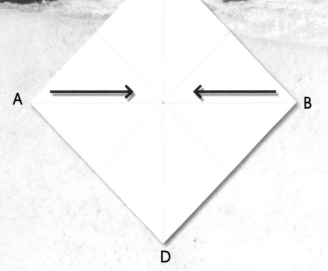

STEP 3:

Using the creases you've just made, collapse and fold up the paper to form a flattened-diamond shape by bringing A in to meet B, and point C down to meet point D.

As you collapse and fold up the paper, it should look like this.

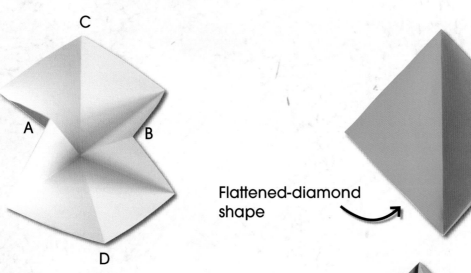

Flattened-diamond shape

STEP 4:

Fold the right-hand point of the diamond into the center of the model, and crease well. (You are only folding the top layer of paper.)

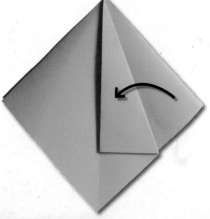

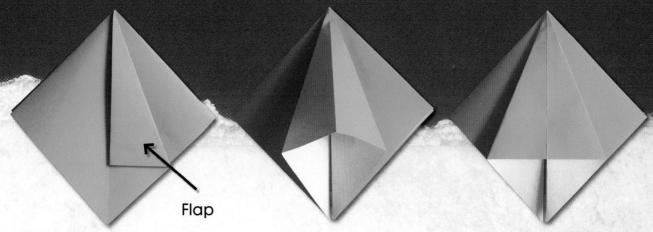

Flap

STEP 5:
Gently open out the flap you've just created to form an upside-down kite shape. Squash the flap flat against the model.

STEP 6:
Now repeat Steps 4 and 5 on the remaining three side points until your model looks like this.

STEP 7:
Rearrange the flaps of your model so it looks like this.

Fold up the bottom of the model along the dotted line, crease hard, and then unfold.

Next, slightly open out your model, and fold each of the small bottom triangles under and inside the model.

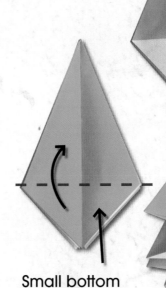

Small bottom triangle

The base of the model will now look like this.

STEP 8:
Finally, stand your tree on a flat surface and arrange the creased edges to get an even, rounded shape.

Your tree seen from above

Origami Santa

It wouldn't be Christmas without the fat, jolly fellow in the red suit. Now you can make your own origami Santa by following these instructions. This is a complicated model with lots of steps. So work slowly and carefully, and you'll soon see Santa emerge from a single sheet of red paper!

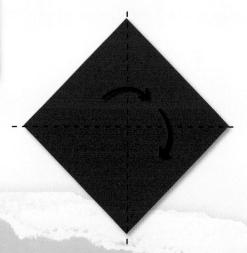

To make an origami Santa, you will need:

One sheet of origami paper that's red on one side and white on the other

(Origami paper is sometimes colored on both sides or white on one side.)

STEP 1:

Place the paper white-side down. Fold the paper in half from side to side, crease, and unfold. Next, fold down from top to bottom, crease, and unfold.

STEP 2:
Fold each side point into the center crease of the model, and crease well.

STEP 3:
Fold the two points back along the dotted lines, and crease.

STEP 4:
Now unfold all the creases you've just made and flatten the paper.

STEP 5:
To make Santa's hands, fold in the two side points of the paper, and crease. Only fold in the points about 1/5 inch (0.5 cm). Then fold each point over again by 1/5 inch (0.5 cm).

STEP 6:
Now fold the paper in half along the dotted line, and crease well.

STEP 7:
Now fold up the bottom point of the model to meet the top edge of the model, and crease well.

STEP 8:

Next, working only with the top layer of paper, fold down the center point to make Santa's face and beard.

Then fold down point A so that a thin edge of the beard can still be seen.

Now fold point A back up along the dotted line and fold it behind itself to create a straight edge.

Finally, fold over the top edge of the face to create a furry brim for Santa's cap.

STEP 9:

Fold up the right-hand side of the model along the dotted line, and crease hard. Then unfold. Repeat on the left-hand side of the model.

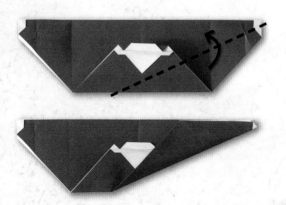

Straight edge

Top edge

Your model should look like this.

STEP 10:

Now fold in the two sides of the model along the dotted lines, and crease hard. Then unfold.

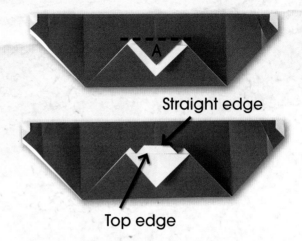

STEP 11:

Next, fold down the two sides of the model, and crease hard.

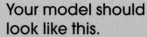

Your model should look like this.

Now repeat on the left-hand side of the model.

STEP 12:

Take hold of the hand on the right-hand side of the model and gently fold back the arm along the black dotted line. As you do this, close up the arm along the white dotted line and flatten it against the model.

STEP 13:

Fold in both sides of the model and crease hard. Your model should now form a triangle with Santa's face in the center.

STEP 14:

Fold the right-hand side of the model backward along the dotted line, and crease hard. Repeat on the left-hand side.

STEP 15:

Gently pull and fold out Santa's arms from inside the body.

Brim of cap

STEP 16:

Crumple the brim of Santa's cap to make it look like fur. Finally, make Santa's feet by folding up the bottom of each leg. Your origami Santa is complete!

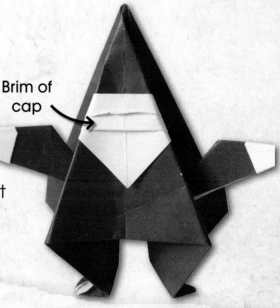

Origami Reindeer

Reindeer are a type of deer that live in the **Arctic** region. They have long antlers and thick, hairy coats that are white and brownish-gray.

In traditional Christmas stories and pictures, however, reindeer are shown with glossy, reddish-brown coats. Some of these mythical creatures even have the ability to fly! The story goes that on Christmas Eve, when Santa sets off from the North Pole to deliver gifts around the world, his sleigh is pulled by a team of eight flying reindeer. These magical reindeer are named Dasher, Dancer, Prancer, Vixen, Comet, Cupid, Donner, and Blitzen.

To make a reindeer, you will need:

A sheet of paper that's any combination
of white, gray, brown, or black

Scissors

(Origami paper is sometimes colored on both sides or white on one side.)

STEP 1:
Place the paper colored-side down. Fold in half, and then unfold.

Fold the top and bottom points into the center crease to make a kite shape, and crease well.

STEP 2:
Now fold the top and bottom points on the left-hand side into the center crease, and crease well.

STEP 3:
Turn the model 90 degrees clockwise. Then fold up the bottom point of the model to meet the top point, crease, and then unfold.

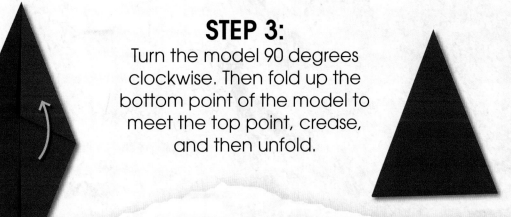

Pocket

Flattened
point

Then repeat on
the left-hand side.

STEP 4:

Open out the top right-hand triangle to create a pocket. Using the creases you've previously made, gently squash and flatten the pocket to make a point.

STEP 5:

Turn the model 90 degrees clockwise and then fold in half along the center crease. Make sure you have a flap of paper pointing toward the left-hand side of the model.

Pointed
flap

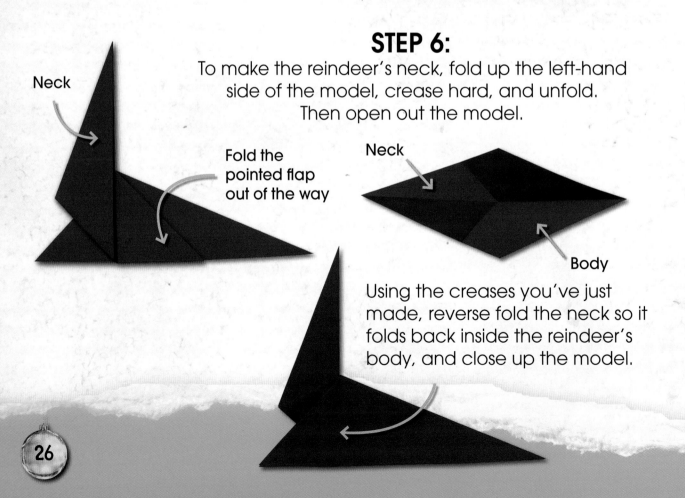

Neck

Fold the
pointed flap
out of the way

STEP 6:

To make the reindeer's neck, fold up the left-hand side of the model, crease hard, and unfold. Then open out the model.

Neck

Body

Using the creases you've just made, reverse fold the neck so it folds back inside the reindeer's body, and close up the model.

STEP 7:

Now fold the pointed flap on the side of the model backward and down to create the reindeer's leg. Repeat on the other side.

Fold down to enclose the neck

Fold tip under

STEP 8:

To make the reindeer's head, fold down the top of the neck, crease hard, and unfold. Open out and flatten the head section. Fold the tip of the head under, then fold down each side of the head around the neck.

STEP 9:

To make the reindeer's antlers, cut up along the dotted line to the fold of the head. Carefully fold up the sliver of paper you've just cut. Gently separate out the layers of paper in the sliver to make the antlers.

Cut along dotted line

Antlers

STEP 10:

Finally, make a cut up the center of the model on the right-hand side to create two points. Fold down each point to make a leg. Then fold out the tip of each leg to make a foot.

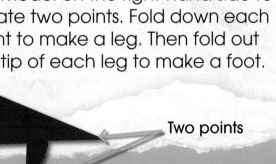

Two points

Origami Christmas Wreath

Wreaths are one of the most popular decorations at Christmas. They are often made from natural materials, such as holly, evergreen branches, berries, and flowers. We see them hung on the front doors of houses and outside stores and offices, too.

This next project shows you how to make a paper wreath to hang inside your home. You can use origami paper or recycle materials such as Christmas wrapping paper and brown paper bags. You can make a wreath to hang on a door, or mini wreaths to decorate a Christmas tree.

A ruler and scissors

A glue pen

Ribbon for hanging

Paper in your choice of colors

(Origami paper is sometimes colored on both sides or white on one side.)

STEP 1:

To make a wreath that measures 7 inches (18 cm) across, you will need 15 pieces of paper each measuring 6 inches by 4 inches (15 cm x 10 cm).

6 inches (15 cm)

4 inches (10 cm)

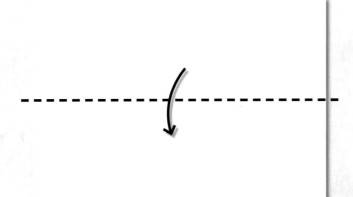

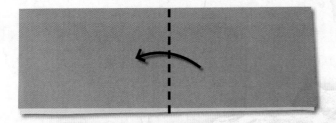

STEP 2:

To make one module of the wreath, place a piece of paper colored-side down, fold it in half along the dotted line, and crease hard. Now fold the model in half again along the dotted line, crease, and then unfold.

STEP 3:
Fold down the right-hand side of the model to meet the center crease you've just made, and crease hard. Then repeat on the left-hand side.

STEP 4:
Turn the model over. Fold up the two bottom corners, and crease.

STEP 5:
Fold up the two flaps at the bottom of the model, and crease. You should now have a triangle.

STEP 6:
Fold the triangle in half. On the left-hand edge of the model, you will now have two pockets. On the lower right-hand side, you will have two points. This is one module of the wreath.

Pockets in here

Two points here

STEP 7:
Repeat Steps 2 to 6 to make 14 more modules, or triangles.

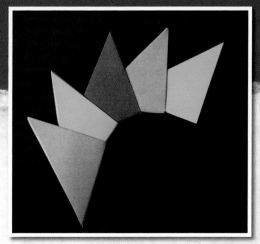

STEP 8:
To begin constructing the wreath, slot the two points of one triangle into the two pockets of another triangle.

STEP 9:
Continue slotting the triangles together.

STEP 10:
Finally, when all the triangles are slotted together, slide the two points of triangle 15 into the pockets of triangle 1 to complete the "circle."

You may want to adjust the positions of the triangles to get them equally spaced and to make the wreath as circular as possible. It's best to do this with the wreath laying on a flat surface. Once you're happy with the wreath's shape, use a glue pen to glue the modules together. Add a ribbon, and your wreath will be ready to hang.

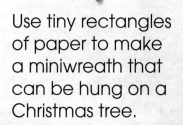

Use tiny rectangles of paper to make a miniwreath that can be hung on a Christmas tree.

Glossary

Arctic (ARK-tik) The northernmost area on Earth, which includes northern parts of Europe, Asia, and North America, the Arctic Ocean, the polar ice cap, and the North Pole.

origami (or-uh-GAH-mee) The art of folding paper into decorative shapes or objects.

sculptures (SKULP-cherz) Works of art that have a shape to them, such as statues or carved objects, and may be made of wood, stone, metal, plaster, or even paper.

symbol (SIM-bul) Something that stands for or represents another thing, such as an important event or person. For example, a cross may be a symbol of Christianity.

unique (yoo-NEEK) One of a kind.

Index

Websites

Due to the changing nature of Internet links, PowerKids Press has developed an online list of websites related to the subject of this book. This site is updated regularly. Please use this link to access the list:

www.powerkidslinks.com/ho/chris